TBug Goes to

Your Travel
Coordinator:
**KATY
VETTA**

ITA

Published by Orange Hat Publishing 2021
ISBN 9781645381969

For information, please contact:

Orange Hat Publishing
www.orangehatpublishing.com
Waukesha, WI

Photography provided by:
Katy Vetta
Clipart.com
Creative Commons
unsplash.com: faruk-kaymak (pg.6), dries-augustyns (pg.10-11),
damiano-baschiera (pg.11), annie-spratt (pg.21), nicolas-hoizey
(pg.27), caleb-miller (pg.26), clay-banks (pg.28), Rahan Shaik (pg.
36), ross-cohen (pg. 42), David Clode (pg.56)

Hi!
I said, "Hello!"
Not up there...
down HERE!

I jump. I fly.
(Some of my relatives
even walk on water.)
Yet, I go unnoticed.
What is THAT about?
I wish humans understood me.
Anyway, T Bug is the name.
Traveling is my game.
I am unique. I am special.
Just like YOU.

Do you love an adventure? Do you wake up every morning, lie around awhile, and wonder what excitement the day has in store? I have explored my yard, my neighborhood, and my community, but I am curious about what else is out there to see and what else is out there to do. I was just wondering . . . any chance you would like to join me? Or rather, any chance you would mind if I joined you? I have several, shall we say, remarkable qualities.

Advantages of Being a Travel Bug

I am small and fit easily into, let's face it . . . ONTO a carry-on bag. I do not make any noise, at least hardly any noise. That's not to say I don't accidentally disturb other travelers, but I generally slip out of sight pretty easily. Travel Security Administration (better know as TSA) employees hardly even notice that I am there. I fall asleep easily on airplanes, in cars, and on trains. I get a little restless on long trips. Seriously, who doesn't? But I can easily fly about to stretch my wings. I require very little food, as compared to humans. And I LOVE TO TRAVEL! It is hard not to be curious about all that I see happening around me, and my eyesight is exceptional, if I do say so myself.

It should not surprise you that I am fit and trim. The insect world can be stressful! All the more reason to take a nice vacation!

Animals are always after us to eat us. Humans can really get worked up when they spot us. One needs to stay on one's toes, ready to scurry, jump, fly, hide, and practice good methods of self-defense. My back legs are particularly helpful, as are my resilin pads, located where my wings meet my thorax. They are made up of rubbery protein for extra bounce.

We're not that much different, you and I. The colors we wear can be useful in helping insects to recognize one another. They can be used to attract a mate or warn predators to stay away. Humans send all kinds of messages with the clothing they wear, don't you agree?

Travelers can only wish for a camera as accurate as the eyes of an insect. With hundreds, maybe even thousands, of lenses focusing on the same picture at exactly the same time, our view of the world is amazing. It is no wonder that I want to see every sight the world has to offer. My night vision, with the aid of simple eyes to detect changes from light to dark and back again, comes in quite handy in new and unfamiliar places.

Think of us as nature's food critics.

Like humans, always looking for the best restaurants at their travel destinations, insects become particularly pleased when they find a good source of food. We dance about with excitement, dancing faster and longer when the food is especially good. You might think of us as food critics!

Insects are also known for their ingenious ways of eating. Humans often search for a straw dispenser. I have no such problem. I carry my reusable, environmentally friendly straw with me at all times. It is called a proboscis and is a long feeding tube, conveniently stored and ready to unroll at a moment's notice.

Remember to stay hydrated on long flights. I sure do.

Let's get better acquainted before we start out.

What is your family like? Sisters, brothers, cousins, good friends? My family is huge! Perhaps you are Italian, German, Latino, Middle Eastern, or likely a combination of several different cultures. Your family name might offer a clue as to where your relatives first started out, or originated. All animal families are called phylums. My particular family name is Arthropod, a term which refers to our jointed limbs. You have jointed limbs too. Arms. Legs. We just have more of them. In fact, you might be surprised to learn who some of our relatives are: crabs, lobsters, shrimp. Most families, even human families, have relatives that are a little hard to explain. I have relatives in Italy. Ask around. Perhaps you do too. Would you mind if we start our travels together in Italy?

FINDING ITALY ON A MAP

It is easy to find Italy on a map if you know where to look. Have you heard the expression "sticks out like a sore thumb"? Well, imagine sticking your boot into the Mediterranean Sea, toe first, heel not far behind. The country of Italy is shaped like a boot with a high heel. Have you spotted it? Certainly hard to miss! It's on the way to just about everywhere in the Mediterranean Sea.

Two large islands are also a part of Italy. They are named Sicily and Sardinia. Sicily is near the pointed toe of the boot. Sardinia is to the west of Italy's peninsula. There are a great many smaller islands that are also a part of Italy . . . about 450 of them, in fact.

Surrounded by water on three sides and protected by the Alps Mountain Range on the fourth side, the country we now know as Italy was easy to get to from Europe to the west, Africa to the south, and Asia to the east and southeast. This made Italy tricky to defend. Of course, crossing the Alps was, and still is, quite a challenge, but you could practically float in from anywhere else.

Water Striders are capable of walking on the surface of water. Now wouldn't THAT come in handy!

Forward, Striders!

Pasta! Pasta! Pasta!

Get 'em!

MOUNTAINS & RIVERS

If you enjoy being near, hiking through, or just gazing at beautiful mountains, Italy will not disappoint. Italy has two long mountain ranges; in fact, nearly half of present-day Italy is made up of mountains. The Alps Mountain Range spreads itself across the top of Italy's boot, from west to east, almost like a thick, furry lining at the top of the boot.

Underneath that furry lining, beginning in the Alps on the far west side where the mountains curve down to meet the Mediterranean Sea, is the source of the Po River. The Po is Italy's longest river, zigzagging across from west to east for over 400 miles and flowing into the Adriatic Sea not far from Venice. The Po River Valley is flat and fertile, making it especially good for farming.

Several other rivers are also located in Italy and often are the reason why cities have been built nearby. Rivers offer a convenient way to move materials, products, and people from place to place.

From the Po River, look down the "leg" of the boot at the many mountain peaks. Practically picking up where the Alps left off, the Apennine Mountains will lead you down the entire length of the boot, from northwest to southeast, until they take a slight turn to the west as they make their way to the toe of the boot and on to the island of Sicily. The Apennines and their ***foothills*** fill most of the peninsula. In a few places, the rocky cliffs stand right up to the Mediterranean Sea. That hasn't stopped the Italian people from building their homes and living on the sides of the mountains. Great examples include Cinque Terre and the Amalfi Coast. They are wonderful places to visit. Don't forget your hiking shoes!

FOOTHILL
noun
A low hill at the base of a mountain or mountain range.

Positano, Amalfi Coast, near Sorrento

Lago di Garda, Sirmione, and the Alps

Three of the largest of more than 1,500 lakes in Italy are also located near the Alps Mountain Range. Grab your lifejacket and paddleboat!! View the amazing Alps from Lago di Como, Lago di Garda, or Lago Maggiore. And you've learned a little Italian! (Lago means lake while di means of.)

GRAB YOUR COMPASS!

Don't forget to grab your compass! I've already got mine. It has been scientifically discovered that members of my arthropod family have an internal compass, rather similar to GPS. Inside of me is a mineral know as magnetite. Magnetoreceptors help insects to determine their location and direction, and these receptors align with the magnetic field of the magni-ficent Earth on which we live.

You may want to let our airplane pilot, or our driver, know that I have this special talent. Are we a team or what? With your compass and my magnetite, at least we know it will be hard to get lost.

If we find the piazza of San Marco in Venice, Italy, I will need to hitch a ride on you, or another unsuspecting tourist, and practice the art of careful *camouflage. Pigeons everywhere! And what do pigeons eat? You betcha! Among other things, they eat INSECTS. They circle overhead and chatter wildly as they search for food sources. Tourists can be seen standing with arms widespread, like a scarecrow, offering a convenient, but temporary, pigeon perch. Do you have food? If not, they will be on their way momentarily. The batting of wings and their cries of disappointment contribute to the general din of this famous piazza.

CAMOUFLAGE
verb
To hide or disguise the presence of (a person, animal, or object) by means of camouflage.

Know your directions!

PIT STOP

You know more Italian than you think you do!
Match the Italian signage to the English translation.

EXAMPLE: Police _____K_____

Theater School _____

Copy Shop _____

Pastry Shop _____

Emergency Exit _____

Ice Cream _____

Restaurant _____

Attention: School _____

Mail Service _____

Open _____

Closed _____

Pizza Restaurant _____

Exit _____

Pharmacy _____

Police (K) | Theater School (I) | Copy Shop (N) | Pastry Shop (J) | Emergency Exit (E) | Ice Cream (F) | Restaurant (H)
Attention: School (C) | Mail Service (L) | Open (M) | Closed (A) | Pizza Restaurant (B) | Exit (G) | Pharmacy (D)

Just Because It's White Doesn't Mean It's Snow!

A special rock has formed and developed over millions of years in the Italian mountains. It is called "marble" and is still being *quarried* in Italy today. There are many enormous buildings in Italy and more statues than you could possibly count. Many, maybe even most, of these were built with some marble.

Marble started out as limestone or dolomite, but it is calcite crystals that give this beautiful rock its sparkle. Limestone and dolomite are *metamorphic*, *sedimentary* rocks, changed by pressure, heat, and water over hundreds of thousands of years. The word "marble" comes from a Greek word meaning "to flash, sparkle, and gleam." The softness of marble makes it easier to carve and less likely to shatter. Light easily passes through the top layers of marble, causing statues to seem almost real.

Lines in the marble and small changes in color are caused by clay, sand, and other materials that have found their way into the rock over time. The colors can help to show you where the marble was found. "Siena" marble will appear yellow and have light-purple, red, blue, or white lines running through it. "Carrara" marble will look very white, but if you look closely, you might see blue and gray lines running through it. Siena and Carrara are two smaller towns in Italy. Michelangelo Buonarroti, a famous artist and sculptor, found some of his marble in the mountains near Carrara. No small task, let me tell you, to pull huge chunks of marble from the mountains and transport them to an artist's studio!

More About Michelangelo Buonarroti

Michelangelo lived in Florence, Italy with his family more than 500 years ago. I like to imagine a 10-year-old Michelangelo running through the streets of Florence. If you get the chance to visit Florence, you will likely see the original *David* statue, created by Michelangelo to portray the young boy that defeated the giant Goliath using only a slingshot as his weapon. Michelangelo completed many amazing works of art, but his *David* has become a symbol of Florence.

This marble statue was carved from what was known as the Duccio Stone. The stone had been rejected by many talented artists because it was damaged and irregular. It took years for Michelangelo to delicately carve *David*. Michelangelo believed that statues actually emerged from the stone. It was the sculptor's job to help them escape.

Like a figure hiding in the marble, I often try to hide among my surroundings. This method is called "camouflage." Being able to blend in makes traveling much easier, especially considering that humans can become quite nervous if they sense an insect in their personal space. It is also helpful to have a tough outer shell called an exoskeleton. This shield offers me a little extra time to consider my options. As a last resort, we have been known to release a foul-smelling chemical, either by biting, stinging, or spraying.

Let's hope that won't be necessary . . .

Did you know there is a beetle named after David's enemy, Goliath? The Goliath Beetle is one of the largest-known insects in the world, weighing as much as some cell phones and growing to over four inches long!

QUARRY
verb
To cut into (rock or ground) to obtain stone or other materials.

METAMORPHIC
adjective
Relating to rock that has undergone transformation by heat, pressure, or other natural causes.

SEDIMENTARY
adjective
Of rock that has formed from sediment deposited by water or air.

Another familiar but unofficial symbol of Florence and the region of Tuscany is the image of a boy named Pinocchio. He was originally a wooden puppet carved by the woodcutter Geppetto. Seems to me to be the same as with Michelangelo. Michelangelo helped David emerge from the stone. Geppetto carved life into Pinocchio.

Italy's Surrounding Seas

The Mediterranean Sea has different names for different regions (wet ones!) surrounding Italy's peninsula. Check the map below for the location of each sea!

- **The Tyrrhenian Sea** (tuh-ree-nee-uhn) is the name given to the water west of the boot.

- **The Adriatic Sea** (ay-dree-a-tik) is the name given to the water east of the boot.

- **The Ionian Sea** (ai-ow-nee-uhn) is the name given to the waters around the heel and toe of the boot.

- **The Ligurian Sea** (luh-gur-ee-uhn) is the name given to the pocket-shaped body of water where Italy meets France.

There are 13 different Italian archipelagos and more than 450 islands. The city of Venice rests on 118 of them.

See if you can spot clusters, or strings, of small islands that are near the Italian peninsula. Having trouble? If you can find a map of Italy on your computer, zoom . . . zoom . . . zoom in! They will start popping up.

Clusters or strings of islands are called archipelagos (aar-kuh-peh-luh-gows). A fun word to say! The Tuscan Archipelago is found to the west of Italy's mainland and close to the French Island of Corsica. There are close to 13 different archipelagos that are a part of Italy for a total of more than 450 islands.

Italy has approximately 1,500 lakes!

Let's Dig a Little Deeper

Perhaps you like playing in the dirt. Maybe you will think about becoming a geologist one day. They have to travel for their work, and Italy is a favorite place for them to explore.

Now hang on to your imagination . . . Geologists are trying to determine if the Apennine Mountains are still growing. Certainly seems that way.

One thing is a sure thing. The Earth's crust is forever changing. These changes cause other changes. Have you ever made a standing chain of dominoes, then pushed the first one into the second and watched them all fall down, each one leaning into the next? Then you might understand what I mean.

Leonardo da Vinci, an Italian inventor and artist, worked in Italy about 600 years ago and made a strange discovery. He found seashell fossils, but nowhere near the sea. He found them buried in limestone in the Apennine Mountains. Geologists tell us that, hundreds of millions of years ago, the Italian peninsula was entirely underwater. That body of water was named "Tethy's Ocean." Layers of sediments on the floor of the shallow ocean hardened into limestone and pushed their way up.

Pushed their way up? How?

Plates underneath the surface of the Earth are always moving: sliding underneath other plates, sometimes colliding with one another. Some plates stretch. Others push. Massive layers of stone rise up above the Earth's surface, creating islands, ***submerging** other islands, building mountain chains, and changing the shape of our continents.

Not that you would notice, of course. It's all happening at a wheel bug's pace, but scientists believe that the island of Sicily, that misshapen ball at the toe of Italy's boot, was once a part of France. Granite is commonly found in Sicily; however, the Apennines are composed mostly of limestone. Put simply, the mountains in Sicily bear more ***resemblance** to the Alps than they do to the Apennines. Could that boot have been lying on its back millions of years ago?

Apulia is the Italian region that forms the "heel" of Italy's boot, and it is believed to have been a part of Africa. Still today, there is scientific evidence, with the help of GPS (Guess that shouldn't surprise us!), to determine motion and direction, helping to prove the theory that Italy's boot is swinging back to the east in ultra slow motion, as if ready to take a kick at the island of Sicily.

SUBMERGE
verb
To put under water.

RESEMBLANCE
noun
A state of being like something or a way in which two or more things are alike.

TIME WILL TELL

Jesus Christ was a *prophet* who became the central figure of the Catholic Church, and the Church's home is Vatican City (a very small country inside a country), located in Rome. For this reason, you will see many statues and paintings devoted to Jesus Christ in Italy.

Time in ancient Rome was measured by whether things happened BEFORE Jesus Christ was born or AFTER Jesus Christ was born. "BC" stands for "Before Christ," and "AD" will refer to years after Christ. "AD" is a term from the Latin language of that time and place and means "Anno Domini."

A new system of labeling time came along about 200 years ago. In the new system, "BCE" stands for "Before the Common Era" and means the same thing as "BC." "CE" stands for "Common Era" and means the same thing as "AD."

PROPHET
noun
One who speaks divinely inspired words that often foretell future events.

Did you know that fossilized insects have also been found, dating back hundreds of millions of years?

Stone fossils might have preserved a wing or crumpled body, but most of the insects dried up and deteriorated. The best and most accurate insect fossils are those found in natural resin. Once trapped in resin, this sticky, transparent, natural substance hardens, encasing, preserving, and protecting the lifeless body trapped inside.

You know what they say . . . we can learn a lot from our elders!

MOUNT VESUVIUS

There are more volcanoes in Italy than in any other country in the world, and some would argue that Mount Vesuvius (which last erupted in 79 CE) is the most famous.

It had been 1,700 years since Mount Vesuvius last erupted. People living nearby had grown somewhat used to the occasional rumblings of minor earthquakes, and to paying little concern. So, it came as a startling and horrifying surprise to people who were living near Mount Vesuvius in 79 CE. The thriving, ancient city of Pompeii sat seven miles southeast of Mount Vesuvius. The people living there were caught off guard by the overwhelming dark cloud and explosion of volcanic rock and ash that would eventually bury their city and all that could not escape.

Pompeii was hit first, and then the wind changed direction. Six *pyroclastic surges* and flows followed. Three of the six continued to bury Pompeii. All six reached the coastal town of Herculaneum, located in the opposite direction from Vesuvius and about 10 miles away from Pompeii. Sixty-five feet, almost seven stories, of ash, debris, and lava buried Herculaneum.

Search and rescue? Terms we hear often these days after a disaster simply did not exist almost 2,000 years ago.

Hundreds of years passed. Eventually, the names of these cities were removed from maps. Farmers began to work what had become very fertile soil, courtesy of volcanic ash, but they were ignorant of what lay deep beneath that soil.

PYROCLASTIC SURGE
noun
A flowing mixture of gas and rock fragments ejected during some volcanic eruptions.

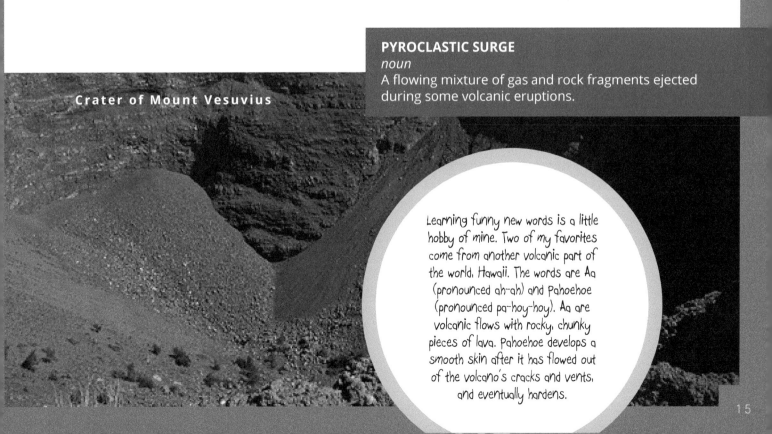

Crater of Mount Vesuvius

Learning funny new words is a little hobby of mine. Two of my favorites come from another volcanic part of the world, Hawaii. The words are Aa (pronounced ah-ah) and Pahoehoe (pronounced pa-hoy-hoy). Aa are volcanic flows with rocky, chunky pieces of lava. Pahoehoe develops a smooth skin after it has flowed out of the volcano's cracks and vents, and eventually hardens.

Hundreds of years later . . .

In 1594, while trying to build a canal, some broken statues, pieces of marble, and parts of paintings were found, but no one made the connection between them and the lost cities.

In 1709, a young prince was trying to build an elaborate villa. His workers discovered buried marble and statues, which could be used to decorate the prince's new home. Still, no one realized what they had found.

In 1738, King Charles III of Spain, ruling Naples and Sicily at that time, also became interested in what might lie underneath. Tunnels were dug, and artwork and statues were hauled out and sent to King Charles' palace.

In 1771, nearly 2,000 years since the famous eruption, the first large home was uncovered, followed by more buildings and more skeletons.

Pompeii Excavations

Even larger strides of discovery began in 1860. A new fellow came to work on the ruins of Pompeii. His name was Giuseppe Fiorelli. He was the first excavator to try his method of restoring remains. Rather than removing skeletons from their hidden, hollow spaces, the spaces were filled with plaster. After hardening, the volcanic rock was chipped away from around the form, coming as near as had ever been possible to creating realistic ***replicas** of the bodies that had been buried there.

In 1984, fewer than 40 years ago, excavators tried pouring hot wax into the cavities where remains were thought to be buried. Coupled with a plaster cast around the wax and then a coat of sturdy ***resin**, far more detailed and transparent replicas of the buried skeletons could be studied and appreciated by travelers like you and me. Work in Pompeii is nowhere near completed, but money has run out, and today the choice must be made between uncovering more remains or trying to protect the already discovered remains that are crumbling away.

Herculaneum Excavations

You remember Herculaneum? That coastal town buried at the same time as Pompeii?

Early in the excavation of Herculaneum, because so few skeletons could be found, everyone breathed a huge sigh of relief. The thought was that most had been able to escape.

Years later, a great many skeletons were discovered in what appears to have been boat stalls. The layers of ash and magma actually pushed the shoreline along the Mediterranean Sea out almost 400 feet, more than the length of a football field. What had once been used as boat storage no longer lay close to the water. On that fateful day in 79 CE, people likely ran toward the sea hoping to escape by boat; however, as the ash found moisture, it thickened, similar to powdered cement when it is mixed with water.

Herculaneum

REPLICA
noun
An exact copy or model of something, especially one on a smaller scale.

RESIN
noun
Any solid or partially solid organic substances that are usually see-through and yellowish or brown. Resin is usually formed in plant secretions and can be used to preserve many different kinds of materials.

VOLCANOES

Many of the islands around Italy rose out of the sea due to tectonic plate movement, discussed a few pages back. Several of these islands rose as volcanoes. Stromboli and Ischia are two examples. Some seemed harmless, so communities grew up around them. A little risky if you ask me, but volcanic ash creates wonderfully fertile soil with lots of minerals that make for a great mud bath or face mask. The heat from beneath the Earth's crust combined with nutrient-rich ash is responsible for popular hot springs that humans (probably even a few insects . . .) love to bathe in. These hot springs attract many tourists and contribute to the lives of workers living in these volcanized locations.

Island of Ischia

Island of Stromboli

Isle of Capri as seen from the mainland coast of Sorrento, Italy

The population remains only in the hundreds on the volcanic island of Stromboli. Keep a safe distance from the continuously active volcano known as "Mount Stromboli." In Carlo Collodi's famous story of Pinocchio, the author named his villain "Mangiafuoco." ("Mangia" is a form of the Italian verb "to eat," and "fuoco" means "fire.") In the Walt Disney version of Pinocchio, the villain's name was changed to "Stromboli." Both names seem accurate for the fearsome and large puppeteer who threatens the wooden Pinocchio with fire and locks him in a cage.

THE BLUE GROTTO

Capri is an example of an island where tectonic plates, weather elements, and surrounding seawaters have carved caves into the mountains. One is particularly popular, called the "Blue Grotto." It may take several hours to find your way to the ferry that circles the Isle of Capri, and once you've actually arrived at the famous Grotto, you will have to climb off the ferry and into a small rowboat. With an experienced guide rowing you toward the seemingly too-small opening of this water-filled cave, you and your fellow passengers, perhaps four to a boat, will have to duck down low, lying as flat as possible to avoid face-planting into the mountain wall, while your deft and capable rower pulls you and your boat into the cave. Described to me as "minutes of pure amazing," the interior of this brilliant blue cave is well worth the trouble. The famous Blue Grotto was at one time a private swimming hole for Emperor Tiberius. Aaaahh! The life of an emperor!

Where Did All the People Come From?

By now, you've noticed that Italy is a boot-shaped peninsula that sits right out there in the middle of the Mediterranean Sea. Hard to miss! Sort of on the way to everywhere else.

It was only natural, I suppose, that people living on all sides of Italy wanted a piece of the action. Perhaps they were looking for a home for their family. Perhaps they were natural explorers. Perhaps they had notions of controlling the land and the people that already lived there. Oftentimes, when things just got crowded in their own countries or territories, people set out to find new lands and set up *colonies*. Starting out small, these colonies often became the larger cities of the future.

Sounds like a potluck supper!

Have you been to a party or picnic where every family has to bring some food to share with the rest of the group? Saves one person from doing all the work, and it also allows everyone to taste and try different things.

A potluck supper is pure heaven for bugs like me. We bring the whole family! Problem is . . . people do not find us so entertaining.

Italian Cuisine

From Here, There, and Everywhere

People traveled far and wide. They came from all sides, bringing their languages, their knowledge, their inventions, their skills, and their traditions along with them. Eventually, the *culture* of Italy grew from everyone's contributions. And once everyone got used to everyone else, they all considered themselves to be 'Romans.'

The Tiber River also runs through Rome, offering a convenient way to bring people and products in and out of this city. Land near a river is usually fertile and highly useful for farming.

PIT STOP

Italians have been at least partially responsible for a great many inventions. Check out some Italian inventions listed here! It's nearly impossible to mention them all!

Eyeglasses

Newspaper

Vespa motor scooter

Jacuzzi

Barometer

Helicopter

Confetti

Blue jeans

Battery

Parachute

Piano

Scuba gear

Telephone

Espresso machine

Paddleboat

Leonardo da Vinci left hundreds of drawings that give us a glimpse into the brilliance of his mind and inventions. The epitome of a Renaissance Man! (See page 51 for more on Renaissance men.)

THE LEGEND OF ROMULUS AND REMUS

The Story Behind the First King of Rome

You have heard of myths, I'm sure. They are tall tales that attempt to explain a phenomenon. *Fuh-naa-muh-naan*. Now that's a tongue twister!

During the earliest history, people looked to natural wonders and worshiped them as gods because, seriously, no one really understood how they came to be. The sun, the moon, the stars, daylight and nighttime, water, war, love. The list goes on and on.

Rhea's father was Numitor, king of a place called "Alba Longa." Numitor's brother, Rhea's Uncle Amulius, seized power away from Numitor. Just to be sure his authority would not be taken away, Amulius wanted to be certain that Numitor would have no family members, especially men, who could claim the kingship. Amulius had all male relatives of Numitor killed and then insisted that Numitor's daughter, Rhea, not be allowed to have children.

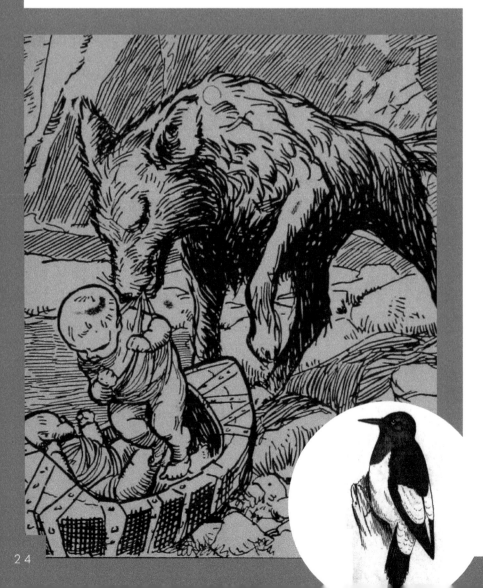

Apparently, Rhea did not get the message, and she gave birth to twin boys, Romulus and Remus. The father of the boys was thought to be Mars, the god of war and agriculture. Amulius was not happy! He took the twin boys to the Tiber River and left them to starve.

Hang on now! This is the crazy part. The river carried the babies to safety. Fortunately for them, along came a she-wolf who offered them her natural milk, and with the help of a woodpecker finding seeds and berries, the two kept the babies alive. Eventually, the wolf and the woodpecker left the boys. Could they have known that someone would come along and take care of them? A shepherd and his wife did just that, raised them, and taught them to be shepherds.

As grown men, the twins learned of their evil Uncle Amulius and saw to it that he was killed. Numitor once again became king.

Not content to wait and inherit Alba Longa, the boys wanted to build a new city where they had been rescued and raised. Romulus wanted it here. Remus wanted it there. In a particularly nasty quarrel, Remus was killed, leaving Romulus to build the new city of Rome on Palatine Hill.

Aventine Hill was the spot that Remus had preferred. Rome eventually expanded across seven hills. Atop each hill, different palaces or grand villas were built.

Let's face it. That's just the myth. More likely, it was farmers and shepherds that appreciated this great location. However, the Romulus and Remus story is more exciting, don't you think? It would make a great movie!

Bring your imagination when you visit the ruins of Rome.

Romulus is also believed to have invented the calendar. The first calendar had only 10 months and allowed for a break of 60 days during the winter. Do your grandparents take several weeks during the winter and find a warmer place to stay? The second king of Rome, named Pompilius, added January and February to the calendar.

A COUNTRY WITHIN A COUNTRY

Vatican City is a very small country inside a country and is located in Rome. In fact, Vatican City is the smallest *sovereign* country in the world, with a population of only 1,000 people inside an area of only 1,100 acres. There are 640 acres in a square mile. You can do the math. With less than two square miles, that is one small country!

Whether your family is Christian or not, if you have the chance to visit Rome, you might also visit Vatican City. Vatican City is famous for its history, and the Pope, as head of the Catholic Church, lives here. Catholic tradition tells us that one of Jesus Christ's closest followers, Simon Peter (later declared a saint), is buried deep below the main altar and is the reason why this spot was chosen for this church.

SOVEREIGN
adjective
Possessing supreme or ultimate power.

TOMB
noun
A large vault, typically an underground one, for burying the dead.

The huge dome you see overlooking Vatican City is part of St. Peter's Basilica and was built to honor Saint Peter. Several others especially important to the Catholic Church have been buried there since then. Perhaps you will get down below to visit these *tombs*. On the other hand, you might have the chance to climb up, and round, and round, and . . . you get the idea. The view from up top is well worth the trip. Try not to bump your head. The staircase spiraling up to the top is more easily tackled if you're willing to lean to the right all the way up and to the left all the way down.

This Church has had a strong voice in Italy for a very long time. Many times, Rome's government struggled to offer strong and effective leadership, and the Church and its leadership stepped in to help out. Countries and individuals who wanted to be on the Church's "good side" often offered gifts of land in exchange for its help. During one long period of time, nearly 1,000 years long, called the "Dark" or "Middle Ages," the Catholic Church controlled vast lands in Italy. That is not the case today, but the Catholic Church still has a lot to say about a great many topics. It is also believed by many that the Catholic Church saved the city of Rome, and certainly preserved its importance, during a "dark" and confused time in Italy's history.

Pope . . . *Joan*?

There have been many popes . . . 266 at last count, beginning with Saint Peter in the year 32 CE. It is thought to be true that all of them have been men, but . . .

Rumor has it that the Catholic Church, a LONG time ago, had a woman sneak through and actually become a Pope. Unheard of! And if it is true, SCANDAL. The legend tells us that Pope Joan disguised herself as a man for many years, but she became a mom, having a baby while she was on a parade route, and surprised everyone, let me tell you!

The Swiss Guard

While you're there, I know you will be a little "caught off guard" by the Swiss Guard, the official soldiers of Vatican City's military. They are the colorful fellows, in the colorful costumes. (Now, there *is* conversation about letting women join the Guard, but not just yet.) Many enjoy trying to make them smile, perhaps even laugh, but it is no simple task. These guys are disciplined!

The Swiss Guard has a long history, and at one time, only soldiers who came from Switzerland were allowed to serve. That is not the case today. Their complicated uniform was designed in the early 1900s. Difficult to make, and hard to wear in the very hot summers, the design continues to be improved upon. New helmets, thought to be available in 2019, are supposed to be made of the same material as PVC pipes, with extra insulation for increased comfort.

Seven great hills of Rome! Seven kings of Rome! I'm beginning to see a pattern. Except for Romulus, who was recognized as the king because he founded the city in 753 BCE, the remaining six kings were elected. They were not the elections that you might see in the town you live in today, and certainly not by secret ballot, but at least people were allowed to speak up and say what they thought. Speaking your mind could get you in a lot of trouble, but at least it was a move in the right direction.

The King and His Lictors

Kings were elected, then expected to serve as king for the rest of their life. The king relied on 12 men, called lictors, who followed the king everywhere in order to protect him. Other officials had lictors too, just not as many as the king. Generally, one could tell how important a person was by the number of bodyguards or lictors walking along with him.

Lictors even followed the king to the baths. Excuse me! Keep in mind that everyone went to the baths together. Private bathrooms were generally not affordable. The symbol of the lictor's power was the fasces, reminding everyone that lictors had the power to "take you out."

LAND HOLDING
noun
A piece of land owned or rented.

PROVINCE
noun
A division of a country or empire.

HEIR
noun
A person inheriting and continuing the legacy of the person that came before.

A person inheriting money, properties, titles, or authority from a parent or governing body.

Lictors stood in a special order around the king. The primus lictor stood right in front of the king, and all the lictors pushed the crowd away from the king. Interesting though, they were not allowed to push mothers out of the way. Something special about mothers! And I agree.

The king and his assembly of advisors had a great deal of power. The king commanded his armies, called "legions." Army generals worked with the king to expand the *land holdings* of the Roman Kingdom, and they did this by conquering *provinces* near and far.

Unfortunately, along with the thirst for new lands came the thirst for power, which oftentimes brought out the worst in people. Plans to do harm to the *heirs* often included violence and torture.

The king also passed laws. He was the judge and the jury in matters of law, but he could not be brought to trial for his own crimes. He appointed all officials. The king remained the king until he died, and all the officials he had appointed left then too. *New king! Fresh start!*

FRIEZE!

"Frees," "freeze," frieze!

Interesting *homonyms*. Watch for stories told above your eyes, but below the ceilings. Look up and learn the *gist* of the story.

Grab your fasces! I've got mine.

HOMONYM
noun
Two or more words that have the same pronunciation/spelling but different meanings

GIST
noun
The essence of a speech or text.

DRESSED FOR SUCCESS

Kings sat on a special chair, known as the curule chair, and they wore a special costume: a purple toga, red shoes, and a white diadem, or simple crown, around their head. Flashy fellows, don't you think?

As far as we know, Romulus brought the fashionable toga to Rome. Rumor has it, the toga was his favorite outfit, and it became equally popular for women. The military also wore togas.

Not happy with the same style for long, people began to try different fabrics, colors, and ways to wrap these long pieces of fabric around themselves. Togas became more expensive and less comfortable. Eventually, togas were used only for very special occasions. Finally, they wore themselves out.

But most styles come back into fashion again and again. If you pay close attention, you may see modern-day wraps and shawls that look much like togas. Maybe you will be invited to a toga party some day and dress as ancient Romans did long ago.

Similar to today's styles, slaves and ordinary citizens wore simple sandals, much like our flip-flops. Soldiers wore stronger sandals with *hobnails* on the soles. Generals returning from successful battles wore *laurel wreaths*, also called diadems, on their heads. Emperors later did the same.

HOBNAIL
noun
A short, heavy-headed nail used to reinforce the soles of boots.

LAUREL WREATH
noun
A round wreath made of connected branches and leaves of the bay laurel, a type of evergreen.

Much later, when the Romans were ruled by emperors, the emperor often set fashion trends. Like today, men shaved their chins, but some had their chins plucked with tweezers by a barber. Emperor Hadrian had an ugly scar on his chin, so he let his beard grow to hide it. Emperor Otto had his entire body plucked of hair. Ouch! He wore a wig to cover his bald head and used moist bread to slow his beard from growing. Whatever the emperor did, men all over the empire did the same to be like him.

Do you like my toga? Just threw it together. Helps me blend in, don't you think?

Notice the ancient curule chair, thought to have been used in ancient Rome. They were uncomfortable, but not by accident. Business of the officials that sat in them was meant to be quick and efficient. The curule chair could be folded up and moved, ready to open again as needed, as the king moved from place to place. Notice the design has not changed much. Nowadays, they're available to most anyone who needs a convenient chair.

Evolution of the Curule Chair

The Silk Road

Distant relatives of mine played an important role in ancient Rome. The Han Empire, today known as China, was responsible for the production of expensive silk, a fabric known for its strong and elastic fibers.

Do you recall where silk comes from? I'll give you a clue. Have you read *Charlotte's Web*? In that case, it was a spider, but most butterflies, moths, and some other insects ***secrete** silk and use it for cocoons, traps (as did that special spider, Charlotte), drag lines (the insect's answer to zip-lining), coverings for their eggs and their prey, and ballooning, a means of letting the wind blow them from place to place.

The Chinese found and bred a special kind of moth that produced a special breed of larvae that produced the finest of silk thread. For thousands of years, and still today, China is considered one of the largest producers of fine silk.

The Silk Road was a very, very, (you get the idea) long road! It was 2,500 miles long, and it linked the Han Empire to the Roman Empire. Caravans of camels carried the silk to Syria, merchants traded silk for things needed back at home, then the silk was carried across the Mediterranean Sea to reach Rome and Greece. More trades were made on the return trip. Talk about a long journey, and I don't think those camels moved all that quickly!

SECRETE
verb
To release or produce.

33

KINGDOM TO REPUBLIC

Clearly, Rome had outgrown its kingdom, wherein one powerful king ran things his own way, and in 509 BCE, a "republic" was formed. In a republic, officials were elected by the people. That is not to say that everyone was heard, but again . . . a big step in that direction.

To be exact, there were two "consuls," and they were in charge of the government and the military and made all important decisions. Sometimes the consuls took turns being the person in charge. "I'll take a month . . . then you take a month." That kind of thing.

Eventually, another group of powerful citizens were chosen to offer advice to the consuls. These "senators" were chosen from wealthier and successful families. All the people in this group were called "patricians." Patricians were the most powerful members of the republic.

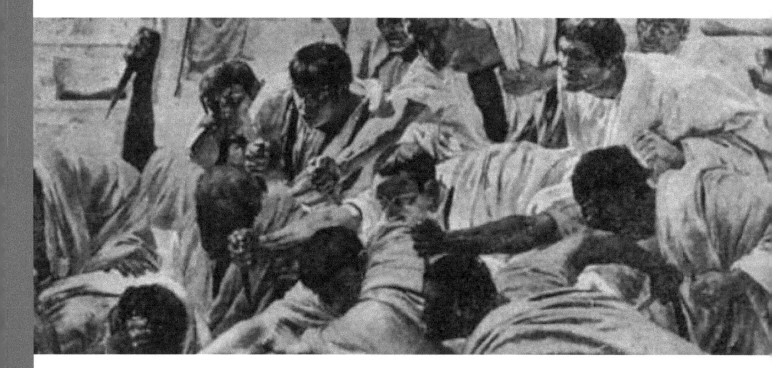

Soon enough, the ordinary families—peasants (small farmers), shepherds, workers, traders, and soldiers—also wanted a say in how things were done. Surely, you and I understand what that feels like. So another layer of government, the tribunal, was formed to represent ordinary citizens and the military. Another name for these ordinary citizens was "plebeians." Even today, you might hear the word "plebes." Just ordinary Joes and Josephines who have valuable ideas. In the Roman Republic, it took another 300 years before they were allowed to vote, but change can be a slow process. Eventually, plebeians were even allowed to become senators.

Some Romans were particularly good at strategizing battles and taking over lands. Some understood government and worked to devise just laws, which would be fair and give everyone something to be happy about. Few Romans managed to do both jobs equally well. To further complicate matters, powerful military generals and powerful rulers often had family members and friends (at least they pretended to be friends, if you know what I mean) who used these close relationships to get their own way, even if their way was not the best way for everyone else.

Perhaps you have heard the expression, "Let's take this outside," meaning this argument is getting out of hand. A fistfight is likely. Take it outside to the Roman Forum, which long ago was the site of Rome's government buildings, shrines, temples, statues, and monuments. Considered by some to be the most celebrated town center in all of history, it was the place where government meetings, processions, elections, and public speeches took place. From famous trials to assassinations, and all means of confrontation, a great many stories of Rome's history include happenings at the Roman Forum. All that remains now are the stories, its ruins, and our imaginations to help us piece together the events that took place there. Best visited on a warm, sunny day, it all has been "left outside." You will have the best view of the Roman Forum from Palatine Hill. Exactly! The spot where Romulus founded this great city so long ago. Looking out to the other side from Palatine Hill, you will get a view of what used to be Circus Maximus. More about that a bit later.

JULIUS CAESAR

Julius Caesar was born in about 100 BCE, became a military general, and eventually was elected as a consul in 60 BCE. He served Italy in the role of consul for 14 years. He was a military genius, an author, and a politician who did much to help the Roman people. Julius also insisted that Rome would be best served by only one *authority*.

AUTHORITY
noun
A person or organization with power or control.

The thought of returning to a supreme ruler . . . a king . . . worried the Roman people. A group of senators, led by a guy named Brutus, along with his brother-in-law, Cassius, decided to take things into their own hands. Seems that's the way things were often done in the Roman Republic. Brutus and Cassius plotted and succeeded in assassinating Julius Caesar in 44 BCE.

Following Caesar's death, Julius Caesar's nephew, Octavian, ready and waiting to take Caesar's place, eventually had to defeat his competitors, Mark Antony and Lepidus, in battle, which left Octavian the strongest man in Rome. There was no line of people waiting to prove him wrong.

PIT STOP

Try saying these Italian words and phrases. They will get you started, anyway. Stress or speak clearest the syllables in capital letters. You will sound like a true Italian!

Phrase	Pronunciation	English Translation
Bella (feminine) Bello (masculine)	BEL-la BEL-lo	Nice/Good/Beautiful.
Mucho bella Mucho bello	Moo-cho bel-la Moo-cho bel-lo	Very beautiful!
Bellisimo	bel-LEES-see-mo	Beautiful.
Bene	Ben-eh	Good/Well
Molto bene	MOL-to BEH-neh	Very well!
Ciào	chee-A-o	Hi/Bye. (casual greeting/goodbye)
Buongiorno	BOO-on jee-OR-no	Good day. (formal greeting/goodbye)
Buonasera	boo-O-na-SEH-ra	Good evening.
Mi scusi	mee SKOO-see	Excuse me.
Non capisco	non ka-PEES-ko	I don't understand.
Mi dispiace	mee dis-pee-A-cheh	I'm sorry.
Mi chiamo	mee kee-A-mo	My name is...
Buon compleanno!	boo-ON kom-pleh-AN-no	Happy Birthday!
Passeggiata	pas-sej-jee-A-ta	a walk/a stroll around town

Phrase	Pronunciation	English Translation
Buonanotte	Boo-o-na-NO-teh	Good night (for before bed)
Si	SEE	Yes
No	No	No (I bet you knew that one!)
Vorrei	vor-REH-ee	I would like...
Per favore	Per fa-VO-reh	Please
Grazie	GRA-zee-eh	Thank you!
Lo sono stanco	Lo soh-no stahn-ko	I am tired.
Lo non sono stanco	Lo nahn soh-no stahn-ko	I am not tired.
Prego	PREH-go	You're welcome.
Delicioso/Deliciosa	Deh-lee-syoh-so/sa	Delicious!
Finito	Fee-NEE-toh	Finished
Buona Fortuna	BWOH-nah For-too-nah	Good luck
Domani	Ieri	Doh-MAH-nee	YEH-ree	Tomorrow	Yesterday
Buon appetito	boo-ON ap-peh-TEE-to	Enjoy your meal.
Perchè?	per-KEH	Why?
Dove...?	DOH-veh	Where is...?
il bagno	eel BA-nee-oh	the bathroom
Parli Inglese	PAR-lee in GLEH-seh?	Do you speak English?
Quanto costa	KWAN-to KOS-ta	How much does this cost?

*As seen overlooking Montepulciano.

Insect communities work in a similar way. Our Queens, or Drones, choose a location for their colonies and decide where the new nests will be built. The workers care for the eggs and collect food. "Majors" are workers that are smaller than queens. "Minors" are the smallest in the colony. Soldiers defend the colony.

Some insects don't buy into this system. They prefer to live on their own and do their own thing. These are called "solitary" insects.

FRIENDLY HILL TOWNS

Some people were happier staying away from all the conflict. They chose instead to live away from cities, to build a quiet life away from battles and crowded confusion. They defended themselves by building walls around their small cities at the tops of hills. From their high perch, they could watch for invaders and protect their families and property. Not only safer, the views from Italy's many hill towns remain quite beautiful. If you ever visit Italy, you must visit at least one hill town. Each one has its own special personality. Some welcome tourists and have many restaurants, shops, and some hotels. Others are quiet and undiscovered, but are happy that you have stopped by. Acquaviva Collecroce is a wonderful example of a quiet hill town.

KINDNESS FINDS YOU IN ACQUAVIVA COLLECROCE

I will never forget the day that we visited Acquaviva Collecroce, located atop a small hill in the Molise region of Italy about an hour's drive from the Adriatic Sea. My husband and I had come to visit the town where his grandfather had grown up. Even now, it is a tiny town of only about 600 people. Evidence of our personal family connections could only be easily found in the crumbling cemetery. Several cracked and worn headstones still carried the Vetta name. We walked the very quiet town, looking for someone who might speak our language. An elderly man walked down the sidewalk. When I asked him if he spoke English, he smiled broadly and replied, "One, two, three, four, five, six, seven, eight, nine, ten." I thanked him and went on my way, but I will never forget the smile that filled his worn and wrinkled face, nor the enthusiasm with which he shared his mastery of the English language.

If you find yourself lost and confused in Italy, ask for help: "Dove" (pronounced "DOH-veh"), which means, "Where is . . . ?" Follow the hand signals. Attempt to speak some Italian. Natives of Italy sure appreciate your effort.

The Meaning Behind the Name:

AQUA
(Water)

VIVA
(Living)

COLLE
(Hill)

CROCE
(Cross)

Loosely Translated:
Living Water of the Cross

The republic had lasted for 500 years, but it was no longer effective. A strong leader was needed, and it seemed that 35-year-old Octavian Caesar was the best man for the job. Yes, the same young fellow who had beaten Mark Antony and Lepidus in battle became Rome's first emperor in 27 BCE.

Emperor Octavian

Octavian was both clever and popular. Octavian respected officials in the Senate, and he left people believing that their comfortable ways were being followed; however, behind the scenes, he ran things his own way. In a wise move, he would not allow anyone to call him "King" or "Emperor," titles that left everyone wondering what his true intentions might be. Instead, he chose the title "Princeps," meaning "first citizen" . . . one of us!

Octavian and his wife Livia lived simply rather than surrounding themselves with riches and wealth. It helped too that no one intended to "fight for it." As you might remember, Octavian had defeated his strongest enemies on the battlefield.

He also brought about great, new programs to feed the poor, to grant citizenship to freed slaves, to raise pay. He not only paid his soldiers well, he treated them with respect. Because of his wise leadership, Octavian became the *gold standard, as far as emperors were concerned. Octavian was so popular that, after he died, he was declared a god. Octavian's reign began a 200-year period of peace, which was called "Pax Romana," and along with the peace came *prosperity.

GOLD STANDARD
noun
The best, most reliable thing of its type.

PROSPERITY
noun
The state of being successful.

BARGE
noun
A flat-bottomed boat for carrying people or products.

Emperor Nero: 54-68 CE

Forty years after Octavian, one particularly corrupt emperor ruled the Roman Empire from 54 to 68 CE. Nero was only 16 years old when he took the throne, and he ruled as emperor for 14 years. Sure seems to me like a lot of power for such a young man!

Granted, Nero often appeared to care about his people. He focused on trading partners and good relationships with other leaders. He saw to it that theaters were built, and he promoted athletic games. On the other hand, Nero was cruel, disrespectful, and used public money to build himself a lavish palace and pleasure *barges*. Nero killed anyone who got in his way, including his wife and his mother.

During his reign, in 64 CE, the Great Fire of Rome destroyed most of this great city. Rumor had it that Nero himself was responsible for the fire, perhaps in hopes of creating space for his new palace. To distract everyone from that rumor, Nero turned the blame on Christians, followers of Jesus Christ. Christianity was unpopular at the time anyway, so Christians were an easy target.

Sooner or later, the army generals, the Senate, and the police force realized what Nero was doing, and he was declared an enemy of the people. Perhaps concerned that he might have to face trial and be punished for his crimes, Nero took his own life in 68 CE.

Following Nero, and illustrating how confused things had become, four different emperors tried to occupy the throne in a single year. The fourth, Emperor Vespasian, ruled wisely, and things fell back into place, at least for a little while.

Emperors came and went, ruling the Roman Empire for more than 1,000 years.

LIVE! LOVE! LAUGH!

Emperors were *dictators*. They had no responsibility to the opinions of the people they governed, but it was worth their while to take care of them anyway. If roads and *aqueducts* were repaired and maintained, if the people had food, if soldiers were disciplined and fair, if taxes were not increased (making it harder for citizens to provide for their families), if crime was dealt with, it all led to a more peaceful and contented population.

Emperors who lived to please themselves, and impress with their luxurious palaces and expensive hobbies, brought about obvious problems. Other emperors agreed that, if they could keep their people happy, busy, and well fed, the people would be far less likely to protest and rebel.

The same is probably true today. Do you like to go to the movies? Do you hang out at the mall now and then? Perhaps spend a lot of time at a community pool or a rec center? Parents love safe places where kids stay busy and hopefully out of trouble.

Similar distractions for young and old alike were needed in the Roman Empire. Circus Maximus was actually first constructed hundreds of years before, but made bigger and better during the Roman Empire. The Colosseum in Rome was built between 72 and 80 CE.

The entertainment was a bit . . . different. Instead of the organized sports you might participate in, the attraction way back when included gladiators fighting one another, and often to the death. Slaves, convicts, and volunteers were oftentimes pitted against one another. Should a slave or criminal manage to defeat their opponent, they might even win their freedom. Sometimes wild animals were thrown into the arena to fight one another. Gruesome? You betcha! Makes you wonder where the animal protection groups were way back then.

Drawing on the Greek example, theaters were also built to entertain the public. Unlike the quiet required at movie theaters and during stage performances today, the crowd typically grew loud and boisterous, with cheering or jeering. Eventually,

DICTATOR
noun
A ruler with total power over a country, especially one who has taken control by force.

AQUEDUCT
noun
An artificial channel for moving water, typically in the form of a bridge across a valley or other gap.

the shows were designed more to shock and awe the audience. Funny, that sounds familiar to present-day concerts, fireworks displays, and circus acts. Maybe things haven't changed as much as we think!

CIRCUS MAXIMUS

Circus Maximus was popular for its chariot races, horse races, gladiatorial contests, elaborate processions, wild animal hunts, and theatrical performances. Circus Maximus is believed to have been the largest circus stadium of all time. It was 621 meters long, nearly seven football fields laid end to end, and 118 meters wide, , nearly equal to two and a half football fields laid side by side. The planning and building of Circus Maximus is believed to have been started by the seventh Roman king, Tarquin the Proud, and was rebuilt and renovated a number of times over the course of the next 1,000 years. The final version was built of stone and could seat 250,000 people. Romans even went so far as to flood their stadiums to reenact naval battles.

At the writing of this book, MetLife Stadium in New Jersey, the NFL football field for the New York Giants and the New York Jets, seated over 82,000 people. The largest sports stadium in the world was in Michigan, at the University of Michigan, seating just over 107,000 people. Neither are even half as large as was the Circus Maximus. Today, a few ruins remain, but the original grounds of Circus Maximus are now a public park.

Need a Bath?

If you're not a fan of crowds, the state-run baths might have been a more desirable choice. These large, and larger still, establishments were popular for their hot and cold pools, exercise areas, reading rooms, massage parlors, shops, and fast-food vendors. Sounds much like the health clubs and resorts that are enjoyed today. All was meant to keep the Roman people content; eventually, these diversions became part of everyday Roman life.

SOMETIMES BIGGER ISN'T BETTER!

The Roman Empire was massive; at its largest in 117 CE, it extended to all the lands touching the Mediterranean Sea, and even far beyond.

Tribes from the fringes of the Empire continued to attack in hopes of increasing their land holdings. The appetite for war seemed nonstop. Money, and more money, was needed to take care of the Empire's population.

In 285 CE, Emperor Diocletian tried to divide the Empire in hope of running things more easily. The western half was called the "Roman Empire" and was ruled from Rome. The eastern half, called the "Byzantine Empire," was ruled from Byzantium, a city far east of Rome on the Black Sea. This worked well for quite a while. Byzantium was a convenient stop on the Silk Road you read about earlier. An important advantage!

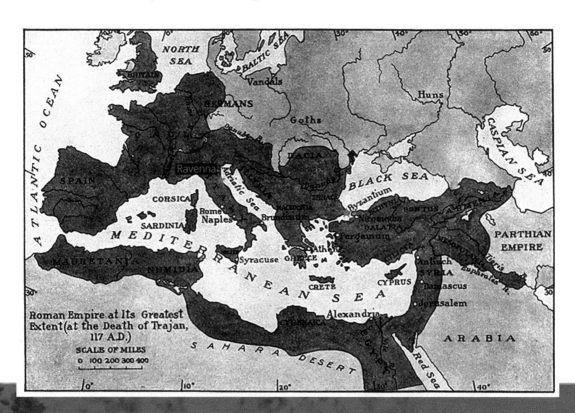

A DIVIDED EMPIRE

Emperor Constantine came along and ruled the Roman Empire from 306 to 337 CE. He changed the name Byzantium to Constantinople. Constantinople became as grand as Rome, then even grander. Gifts of land and money were sent to the government of Constantinople rather than to Rome. Schools were built, and products for trading sprung up in the eastern capital, leaving Rome and the west with less and less to help their city thrive.

Ready to try just about anything, the *court* of the western Roman Empire picked up and moved 200 miles north to the town of Ravenna, on the eastern coast of the boot, so as to be closer to Constantinople and more easily protected.

After claiming he had seen a vision of a flaming cross in the sky, and before his death in 313 CE, Emperor Constantine was *baptized* a Christian and ordered an end to the *persecution* of these believers. Not only could Christians come out of hiding, any that were willing to convert to Christianity received rewards and jobs for their efforts.

As Christianity became more popular, people of the Roman Empire turned against those of the Jewish faith and decided that Jews would have to leave Europe. Why is it that people cannot just agree to disagree?

Jewish people often moved to Arab countries (current-day Middle East), where people tended to practice the Islamic faith. Unfortunately, Jews were not treated fairly there either. They had to pay higher taxes and were not allowed to protect themselves with weapons, but there was at least more acceptance of their religious beliefs. They were allowed to worship as they pleased.

The Byzantine Empire combined its knowledge of the Greek culture with the views of the Christian faith and formed its own version of Christianity, the Greek Orthodox Church. The centers of power in Constantinople and Rome parted ways over religious disagreements in 1054 CE.

COURT
noun
Includes the leadership, its family, and the official persons and offices that guide, manage, and handle its people, usually housed nearby one another.

BAPTIZE
noun
The religious act of sprinkling water onto a person's forehead or of immersion in water, symbolizing that the person has been made new and pure.

PERSECUTION
noun
The aggravation, irritation, punishment, or harassment of a particular group of people.

REFUGE
noun
A condition of being safe or sheltered from pursuit, danger, or trouble.

ROMAN CATACOMBS

Many emperors considered themselves to be gods, or the nearest thing to them . . . a "bridge to the gods," and they wanted to be treated like gods. At the very least, they expected their people to follow the religion that the emperor chose. Those that refused could be severely punished, perhaps even killed, for having a different opinion.

Christians found a safe *refuge* in catacombs, underground burial sites. By law, burial sites had to be outside the city, and they were considered sacred . . . untouchable. Tradition, with a little fear mixed in (okay, sometimes a lot of fear) offered Christians a safe, however uncomfortable, place to hide and worship in peace.

As long as you're not spooked by burial places, you should think about visiting the Roman catacombs. Some pretty amazing artwork on the walls of these tunneled burial grounds dates back to 200 CE and gives us a glimpse into people's lives and what was most important to them so long ago.

**Everything had become a bit *discombobulated*.
Just saying that word describes its definition!**

A weak Rome was a perfect target. No end to the power struggles! Rome just had fewer ways with which to fight back. It was hard to come up with enough local soldiers. Foreign soldiers from the north came looking for work, but their ***loyalty** was always a question.

LOYALTY
noun
A strong feeling of support or allegiance.

EXTRA! EXTRA!
SOLDIERS WANTED!

Learn new skills on the job;
Retire with land and money;
BYO (Bring your own . . .) breastplates and shields.

PROVIDED:
spears, daggers, short swords, battering rams,
stone-throwing machines

BARBARIANS

The name given to tribes from outside the Empire who spoke different languages was "barbarian." The word began in the Greek culture and referred to the "gibberish," or so it seemed, spoken by people from foreign places. "Bar . . . bar . . . bar . . ." was commonly used to describe the stuttering of people struggling to learn a new language. Eventually, this word began being used as an ordinary Latin word for "soldier."

In 410 CE, another of these pesky barbarian tribes, the Visigoths, led by a king named Alaric, reached and sacked Rome, which no one in 800 years had managed to do.

If you're a football fan, perhaps you've heard the term "sacked." It describes what happens to a quarterback when his front line of blockers lets the opposing team through. The opposing players hope to tackle the quarterback, or at least push him back as far as they can, before he has a chance to get rid of the ball. If they can push the quarterback behind the *line of scrimmage*, the result is a "sack." The quarterback often rises a bit slowly, reeling from the hard hit. Similarly, each "sack" left Rome more weak and confused.

Many tribes originated in a large area known as Germania, located north of present-day Italy, and their goal was to take over Rome.

LINE OF SCRIMMAGE
noun
The imaginary line separating the teams at the beginning of a play

MIGRATION
noun
Movement from one country or place to another.

NEGOTIATOR
noun
A person who helps to bring about an agreement.

I find it nearly impossible to keep all of the warring tribes straight. Who came from where? Why did they come? Where did they finally settle down and make themselves at home? A map of their *migration* reminds me of a tangle of yarn, crisscrossing and winding all over the continent of Europe.

Goths, Visigoths, Ostrogoths . . . and that's just the Goths!

The Gauls, the Huns, the Saracens, the Lombards, the Franks. They came. They fought. Often they conquered. All the while, the Roman emperor hoped to straighten out the tangles and unite the East again with the West. Good luck with that!

Fortunately, the Catholic Church remained in Rome. Actually, their power grew during this time. One particular leader, Pope Leo, later dubbed "Peter the Great," rode out to meet the ferocious tribal leader Attila the Hun and his powerful army in 452 CE. Leo must have been a great *negotiator* because he talked them out of invading Rome yet again. Pope Leo was the first pope to be called "The Great."

Two of the stronger German tribes made their sure way into the Roman Empire, both East and West. The Lombards were more vicious and violent; the Franks were more reasonable.

PIT STOP

Know your numbers!
Practice counting in Italian! Try out your best
Italian accent. Have fun!

Number	Pronunciation	English Translation
Uno	OO-no	One
Due	DOO-eh	Two
Tre	TREH	Three
Quattro	KWAT-tro	Four
Cinque	CHIN-kweh	Five
Sei	SEH-ee	Six
Sette	SET-teh	Seven
Otto	OT-to	Eight

Phrase	Pronunciation	English Translation
Nove	NO-veh	Nine
Dieci	Dee-EH-chee	Ten
Undici	OON-dee-chee	Eleven
Dodici	DO-dee-chee	Twelve
Tredici	TREH-dee-chee	Thirteen
Quattrodici	KWAT-tor-dee-chee	Fourteen
Quindici	KWIN-dee-chee	Fifteen
Sedici	SEH-dee-chee	Sixteen
Diciassette	dee-chas-SET-teh	Seventeen
Diciotto	dee-CHOT-to	Eighteen
Diciannove	dee-chan-NO-veh	Nineteen
Venti	VEN-tee	Twenty

1. Double consonants are held longer on your tongue. Try saying *pizza*.

2. Vowel sounds are more consistent in the Italian language:

"A" is pronounced *ah* | "E" is pronounced *eh* | "I" is pronounce *ee* | "O" is pronounced *oh* | "U" is pronounced *oo*

"Ch" has a hard *c* sound. "C" alone, but followed by an "I", has a *ch* sound. "Gh" has a hard *g* sound. "G", followed by a vowel, has a soft *g* sound. "Gn" has a *nyo*.

CHARLEMAGNE

Charlemagne was a famous Frank general. He was King of the Franks from 768 to 774 CE. He then defeated the Lombards, so he was made King of the Lombards too from 774 to 800 CE. Yes, lots and lots of fighting going on!

Charlemagne watched out for the Church, returning lands to the Church that had been lost to the Lombards during battle. Eventually, and so grateful for Charlemagne's leadership and fairness, the Church crowned Charlemagne the first Germanic Emperor of Rome in 800 CE.

There was still some disagreement as to who would have the final say, but compared to the rough times of the past, Charlemagne was a welcome change. Charlemagne's main goal was to unite the Western Roman Empire. He came as close as anyone could, or ever would. Shortly after his death, the Western Empire was divided into France, Italy, and Germany. Conveniently, Charlemagne had three grandsons to run them.

ORDER	SECLUDED
noun	*adjective*
A group of people united in a formal way.	(Of a place) not seen or visited by many people; sheltered and private.

Charlemagne was one of only a few bright spots. This long stretch in history between 500 CE and 1500 CE has become known as the "Dark Ages" or "Middle Ages."

During this time, different ***orders** of monks formed. At first, these groups of like-minded men and women ***secluded** themselves in prayer as they searched for answers to life's difficult problems. Eventually, they built monasteries to live in and worked to help maintain them while they studied, copied great works of literature (No copy machines handy!) and prayed for guidance.

Some monks believed that knowledge could be a bad thing. They thought that people would be more content, more orderly, happier, I guess, if they were not allowed to know too much.

What do YOU think?

I want to be a Renaissance Bug. You may have noticed . . . I "wear many hats!"

And that brings us to the Renaissance . . .

Have you heard the term "Renaissance Man"?

Unfortunately, there were not many Renaissance Women so long ago. That does not mean that they weren't there . . . they just weren't recognized. Particularly in less wealthy families, where everyone in the family needed to roll up their sleeves and pitch in, women worked long and hard to help in their family businesses. Many were talented women who actually ran the family businesses.

Today, this term is used to describe men and women who have a variety of talents and interests and try to learn about, and practice, all of them.

With no strong leadership in the Roman Empire, each city rebuilt itself using the resources unique to their cities. They formed "city-states." People good at leading emerged in these cities and helped the people decide what kind of government structure their own cities would follow.

Cities along the coastline became trading cities. The city of Venice had an added advantage. It was near enough to Constantinople, formerly called Byzantium (home of the Eastern Roman Empire), to trade through Constantinople to the many countries beyond. Other cities relied on farming or manufacturing. Milan was one of the manufacturing cities.

What are YOUR talents? There are more than you probably realize. YOU could be the next Renaissance kid!

FLORENCE

The Italian city of Florence was able to *****fly under the radar** (Just like ME!) because it was far enough away from both Rome and Constantinople, yet somewhat harder to get to with the Apennine Mountains in the way.

Cosimo (pronounced just like it sounds) Medici was one of those talented leaders I mentioned earlier. Cosimo became nicknamed "Father of His Country." His name is still easily recognized in the city of Florence. After Cosimo, his grandson Lorenzo continued leading Florence to greatness, earning the title "Lorenzo the Magnificent."

Cosimo and Lorenzo were eager to encourage young talent. Unlike most fancy gatherings, the first visitors to arrive at the Medici home were given seats of honor next to their host. They weren't seated according to their rank. They were encouraged to join in as equals. Lorenzo founded the Academy in Florence. It is still an important center of learning.

One of those talented, young artists was Michelangelo Buonarotti, who was, of course, a Renaissance Man. Painter, sculptor, architect, and poet, just to name a few of his gifts, Michelangelo carved the famous statue of *David*.

As the story goes, David struck down the much larger and fiercer Goliath with a simple slingshot as his only weapon. The original statue of David is protected inside the Accademia in Florence. Several of its copies can be found all over Florence, and *David* stands as a symbol of great strength for the Florentine people.

Kind and wise leadership allowed Florentines to read, learn, create, invent, and pursue their passions.

There were plenty of people who had no patience for this idea of "free thinking." Those people depended on the old ideas. They did not want their authority questioned. They did not want new ideas replacing comfortable traditions.

Because of this, another type of war took place.

One monk, Savonarola, wanted the population to return to religion and charitable work. Savonarola made a "fiery" statement when he lit a bonfire in the streets of Florence in hopes of wiping out the artwork, books, instruments, cosmetics, and all else that he determined to be evil.

The coolest thing, in my low-ly (just a little bug humor) estimation, is how all of the problems of the Dark, Middle Ages led to so much excitement, fascinating inventions, and artwork, still teaching and affecting us 800 years later.

You might want to read more about the artists, architects, inventors, and great thinkers of the Renaissance: Michelangelo, Brunelleschi, Raphael, Leonardo da Vinci, Donatello, Bramante, and Machiavelli, just to name a few.

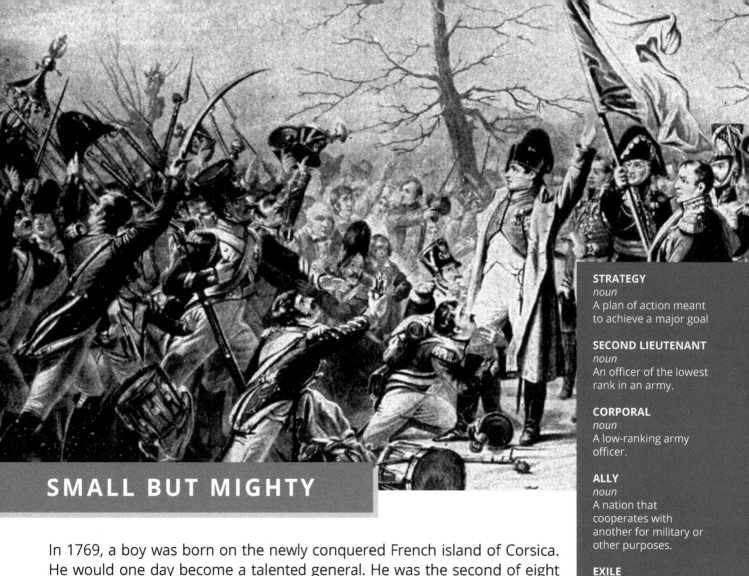

SMALL BUT MIGHTY

In 1769, a boy was born on the newly conquered French island of Corsica. He would one day become a talented general. He was the second of eight children, born to Italian parents, and he was sent to the military academy at only ten years old. Even as a very young man, Napoleon Bonaparte had a gift for war ***strategy**, and he was a huge help to France. Small in size, but with huge determination and an intelligent military mind, he went on to squash revolts in most of the surrounding countries.

At age 17, he became a ***second lieutenant** and was nicknamed "Little ***Corporal."** Over time, his ambition for power became nonstop. He didn't wait long to be given a higher position. In fact, he declared himself "Consul for Life" in 1799 as well as "Emperor of France" and "King of Italy" in 1804.

With his vast power, he was able to give "gifts" of regions and titles of importance to go along with them. In 1810, he named his infant son "King of Rome." The little boy remained "King of Italy" until the age of three.

I think that was taking things a little too far, don't you?

Fearing an invasion from Napoleon in Moscow, the Russians burned down villages and most of Moscow, hoping to deprive Napoleon and his men of food and shelter for his troops when they arrived. Seems it worked! The story goes that Napoleon saw the situation, then disguised himself as a peasant and snuck out of town.

Things were falling apart for Bonaparte!

After that embarrassment in 1812, Napoleon was forced to leave France in 1814, when *allied* forces invaded and *exiled* Napoleon to the island of Elba, practically swimming distance from Italy's mainland. Of course, one would have to be a particularly strong swimmer.

Napoleon ruled the small island of Elba for the French until he escaped back to France again in 1815. The British later exiled Napoleon to the island of Saint Helena, much farther away, off the coast of Africa, where he lived for another six years.

Whether or not one agreed with Napoleon can be argued, but his ideas, named the Napoleonic Code, remain a part of our modern legal systems even after all of this time.

Elba Island

TUSCAN ARCHIPELAGO

Not only is this a great example of an archipelago, but each island comes with its own story.

Remember that long ago, mysterious phenomenon, and the need to explain them, grew into stories called "myths." The myth explaining the Tuscan Archipelago tells us that this string of islands was created when Venus, the goddess of love and beauty, was coming out of the water and dropped her necklace into the Tyrrhenian Sea. She scrambled to collect her precious pearls, but seven of them were left in the sea, and, you guessed it, they became the islands of the Tuscan Archipelago.

One of these small islands is named Montecristo. Perhaps you've heard the story *The Count of Monte Cristo*. This famous and exciting story was first written in 1844. It is hard to know how much of the story is factual, but the book, movies, miniseries, musicals, plays, and rewrites of the book have been created all based on the story of a sailor named Edmond Dantès who was wrongly accused of, and thrown in prison unfairly for, aiding Napoleon in his escape from Elba.

Elba Island

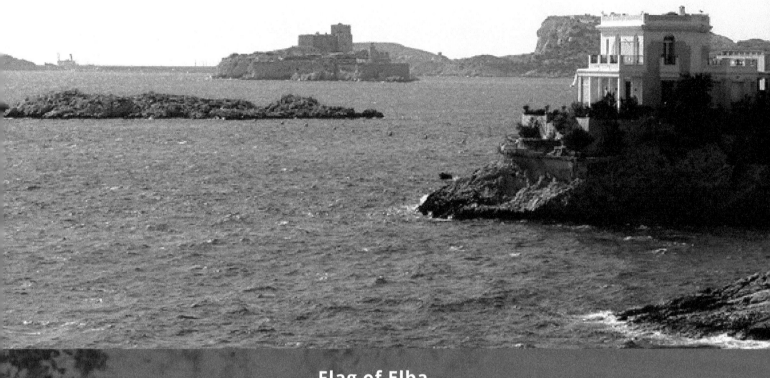

Frioul Archipelago
*Off the coast of Marseille, France

Flag of Elba

How about this great flag? Napoleon Bonaparte designed the flag for the island of Elba. Three golden bees pictured on a banner of red against a background of white. People disagree over the symbolism of the red banner, but the bees are thought to represent unity and hard work. Obviously necessary in a bee's society! Another thought . . . Elba had already had three rulers. Napoleon was the fourth and the one who would unite all under one flag. Cool flag, in my "arthropodic" opinion, even if Napoleon did not last long on Elba.

Elba Island

SPEAKING OF BEES...

If we have time, and if we travel in the fall, we should consider making it to the annual Honey Festival in the town of Sortino on the island of Sicily. The varieties of honey will astound you. Always in great demand is the "millefiori," translated, "thousand flowers."

The Italian honeybee, originally from the central and southern mainland of Italy, is known to be laid-back, but hardworking, much like the Italian people. These bees tend to be enthusiastic, gentle, unlikely to swarm, clean, and healthy.

I'm so very proud of these great relatives of mine!

Added to all of that, Italian honeybee queens lay roughly 1,500 new eggs every 24 hours between April and July. Whoa!

For these obvious reasons, in the 1970s and 1980s, the Italian honeybee was "all the rage." The great popularity of the Italian honeybee nearly caused the Sicilian black bee to become extinct. One particularly concerned *apiarist* moved the black bees to small islands off the northeast coast of Sicily, where they could again become active and productive without being disturbed by other breeds of bees.

APIARIST
noun
A beekeeper.

Happy bees! Happy farmers! And some consider the black bee honey to be the tastiest found just about anywhere.

It's not all about the honey...

BROOD
noun
A family
of young
animals.

Maintaining the hive and protecting the ***brood** is no small task. Honeybees produce a resin called "propolis" when they mix evergreen tree sap with their beeswax and other discharges. Strong and sturdy bees use propolis for mending air pockets in their hives. Ancient civilizations used propolis on wounds and tumors to help them heal. Egyptians used propolis to preserve mummies.

Let's keep an eye out for royal jelly. Bees transfer this jelly from their heads to the queen's hive, helping her to grow larger, to live longer, and to develop reproductive organs. Like breast milk for babies, royal jelly is fed to bees in the larvae stage and is thought to give them a healthy start. Humans today add organic royal jelly to their yogurt, smoothies, salads, and drinks. *What's good for the queen . . .*

SAINT ROSALIA OF PALERMO

Special to Sicily, particularly to the city of Palermo, is the story of their patron saint. The term "saint" suggests a special connection to a world that humans don't entirely understand, often inspired by a mysterious "phenomenon," as we mentioned earlier. Patron saints have been chosen to represent places, occupations, causes, even families. You get the idea? They are honored as special protectors, insiders, who can offer people extra hope when they become discouraged.

Sitting out there, oftentimes unprotected, in the middle of the Mediterranean Sea, Sicily saw many different rulers try to run the show over hundreds of years. Just before one of these groups, the Normans, stormed in, the Arabs (also called "Saracens") had been in charge. They built magnificent palaces and brought much of their artwork and practices to the island of Sicily. One of these practices was "harems," several women connected in one way or another to a single man. Wives, servants, relatives . . . these harems could be rather large. The Normans *inherited* this Arab tradition.

INHERIT
verb
To receive (money, property, or a title) as an heir after the death of the previous holder.

PLAGUE
noun
A contagious disease that includes fever and infection of the lungs.

King Roger headed up the Normans in Sicily. Roger's niece, Rosalia, only 12 or 13 years old at the time, was part of his harem. While hunting one day on Mount Pellegrino, near Palermo, Sicily, Roger was attacked by a wild lion. (Is there any other kind?) Fortunately, Roger's guest, Prince Baldwin, was there to fight off the lion and save Roger's life. Lesson learned? Don't go hunting alone! In gratitude for saving his life, King Roger offered Prince Baldwin anything he had. The prince chose his beautiful niece, Rosalia, and asked that she become his wife. Or one of them, anyway. Try as they might, Rosalia's family could not convince her that this was a good plan. Rebelling, Rosalia cut off her beautiful hair and ran away to a cave in the nearby mountains. She is believed to have lived there alone the rest of her life and devoted her life to her god.

Fast-forward 300 years later . . . In 1624, a terrible ***plague*** fell on Sicily. Many died from the terrible disease. The people of Sicily prayed night and day to their saints and gods, yet the plague continued.

Meanwhile, a soap maker named Vincenzo Bonelli was out walking on Mount Pellegrino when Rosalia appeared to him as if in a dream. She led Vincenzo to her cave and to the remains of her life. She asked Vincenzo to arrange for a proper burial, and in exchange, she would end the plague. It took some convincing, but the city officials finally agreed to a proper funeral and a procession of Rosalia's remains through the city of Palermo. Presto! The plague ended.

Since that time, Rosalia has been honored as the patron saint of Palermo. Rosalia's feast day is September 4th, but an annual celebration is held every year in the middle of July. Rose became a common name for daughters in Sicily.

Patron saints and their miraculous stories are common all over the world.

Sicily at Mount Pellegrino,
overlooking Palermo

PIT STOP

Scavenger Hunt!
Take this game with you to a museum. You'll be surprised at how many of these items have found their way into history and artwork.

Give yourself one point for finding or identifying:
(First one to 10 points wins.)

☐ Flag of Italy

☐ Toga

☐ Curule Chair

☐ Laurel Wreath

☐ Pinocchio

☐ Marble from Siena

light-purple, red, blue, or white lines running through it.

☐ Marble from Carrara

Very white with faint blue and gray lines running through it.

☐ Volcano

Name it for TWO points.

☐ Island

Name it for TWO points.

☐ Ruin

Name it for TWO points.

☐ Soldier from the Swiss Guard

(No laughing!)

☐ Large hole in the ceiling

Hint: it's inside a famous building in Rome

☐ Fasces

☐ Ferrari Emblem (Prancing Horse)

ENZO FERRARI

If we have time to explore the city of Bologna, we should buzz on over to Maranello, where the famous Ferrari automobile plant, and all things Ferrari for that matter, will offer auto racing lovers a day they won't soon forget.

During World War I, a good friend and Italian fighter pilot named Francesco Baracca was killed, but he inspired Enzo, and the prancing horse that Baracca had created for his family's ***crest** was offered to Enzo Ferrari. In Baracca's honor, Enzo gave his life's work, and the automobiles he helped to create, this symbol, or more aptly, this "brand," called a "marque" in the racing world. Today, all things Ferrari are displayed grandly in Maranello, Italy, including a huge statue of the prancing horse.

CREST/COAT OF ARMS
noun
A shield with symbols and figures that represent a family, person, a group, or other organization.

FORMULA ONE

Ferrari is one of several European auto manufacturers that has built the Formula One auto racing competition over the past 100 years.

"Formula" refers to the set of rules that apply to these races. "Grand Prix" refers to the grand prize that is awarded to both drivers and *constructors* for points won over a series of several races.

CONSTRUCTORS
noun
People or corporations which design key parts of the Formula One cars that compete.

Achieving the standards set by Formula One is no small feat! The drivers of these vehicles, with seats that conform nearly perfectly to each individual driver, have their work cut out for them on race day. In preparing for each race, the engineers and technicians work diligently behind the scenes to meet every standard and to push every engine and component of their cars to their absolute limit without allowing them to fail.

At one time, auto racing was terribly, often tragically, dangerous for lack of rules and regulations. Today, even with stricter guidelines, race car driving remains a challenging and perilous sport. Continually, safety features are built in to protect the driver and the fans. The "pits" are not only used for "pit stops," on the spot repairs to the cars, but also as "time-out chairs" for drivers who tend to stretch, and break, the strict rules of auto racing.

One race remains an Italian tradition. It is the "Mille Miglia" (Thousand Miles), or MM. This major race was run in Italy 24 times between 1927 and 1957. Not as much a race anymore as it is a parade of sorts, the Mille Miglia course may take several days to run and only includes cars that were built before 1957.

WHAT'S THE BUZZ?

Earplugs are a great suggestion should you have the chance to attend an auto racing event. I flew over the Indy 500 Grand Prix race one time. The seriously loud thrum of the cars as they speed around the track is a sound both hard to describe and hard to forget.

Although there are actually more than 100,000 kinds of flies, which might leave you wondering how one measures such a phenomenon, some claim that flies are among the fastest insects alive. And yes, that does account for the buzzing you will hear even when you cannot even see these annoying little creatures about you. Their wings beat at a rate of 200 times per SECOND. Translated, that becomes roughly four and a half miles per hour. Most of us can't even run that fast!

Two other features offer these little guys a "heads-up," or should we say a "hairs-up"? Hairs on their bodies act like motion sensors, so they have just that much extra time to react and escape your fly swatter. I've already pointed out their ability to see with each of their thousands of eye lenses pointed in slightly different directions.

It's no wonder they can be so difficult to take down!

Oh no! I nearly forgot!

While we're on the topic of buzzing, and no, I'm not going to tell you more about my relatives (at least not for now), when you visit the cities of Italy, it will be hard to ignore the activity and the NOISE of all the motorbike engines. Vespa is a popular brand, and it is the Italian word for wasp. Okay. Okay. I promise I wasn't talking about my family!

Even the sidewalks are not safe! The motorbikes are more compact and easily sidle up to pedestrians as they clamor to pass the automobiles and push to the front of the line, ready and waiting for the stoplights to turn green.

Stay on the lookout! Some say that traffic rules in Italy are only a suggestion...

MARIA MONTESSORI

Maria Montessori is famous for her work building Montessori Schools, but that is only one of her many accomplishments.

She was born in 1870 in an Italian town named Chiaravalle, near the Adriatic Sea and to the east of Florence. Her father, Alessandro, was an official for the Italian government and worked in a tobacco factory. Maria's mother was educated even though it was unusual for women to receive much schooling. Maria's father disagreed with Maria's mother and discouraged Maria from studying and going to school, but it seems that Maria and her mother were determined women.

Maria was three years old when her family moved to Florence. They moved to Rome when she was five. Maria began formal school when she was six years old; however, she was not noticed as having special talent until she was about 13. By then, she was studying math, algebra, history, sciences, and two foreign languages, among other subjects.

At first, she wanted to be an engineer, but by the time she was 20 years old, she had decided to study medicine. This was extremely unusual for a woman. Because of her ambition, she was teased by other students and her teachers. Male students were not comfortable working alongside a woman, so Maria had to study *cadavers* after the men had gone home. Maria graduated from the University of Rome in 1896 and became an expert in *pediatrics.*

CADAVER
noun
A dead body.

PEDIATRICS
noun
The branch of medicine dealing with children and their diseases.

Between 1896 and 1901, Maria worked with children with mental disabilities. Maria helped to start a school that would train teachers to work with these children. The Montessori system of teaching was developed during these years and successfully taught children who were thought to be unteachable and unreachable.

ITALIAN TENORS

How low can you go? How high can you fly? How much does your voice weigh? What is your tessitura? Can you find your passagio? I can never remember where I put mine . . .

The world of opera is not for everyone, but two Italians have brought so much to the world of opera! Luciano Pavarotti, born and died in the Italian town of Modena, and Andrea Bocelli, born in his hometown of Lajatico in the Tuscany region. Bocelli is fortunately still with us to inspire with his stunning singing voice.

Singing is not just reserved for the shower! "Opera" is theater set almost entirely to music, and voices of every range, or "tessitura," are needed. Eight voice types have been identified. Four are more likely assigned to females, and the other four to male voices, but even this is not a hard and fast rule. Every voice is different. Kind of like a fingerprint. The heavier and more dramatic one's voice is, the greater is its "weight."

For female voices, the ranges, from lowest to highest, are Contralto, Alto, Mezzo (middle) Soprano, and Soprano. For male voices, again from lowest to highest, the ranges are named Bass, Baritone, Tenor, and Countertenor. As with most sports, and many subjects, coaches are needed to teach and encourage us to stretch our talents and reach a little higher, or in the case of music, a little lower. Trying too much too soon can be both disappointing and cause injury. Song artists take great pains to protect their voices. Pavarotti's greatest fear was catching a cold. Andrea Bocelli protects his voice by remaining completely silent for 24 straight hours prior to performances.

"Passagio" is the Italian word for "bridge." As you sing these simple words to the notes of a scale, do-re-mi-fa-so-la-ti-do, and repeat them as you sing higher or lower, you will likely find your passagio. It is the point at which certain notes "crack" during the effort. That crack is the passagio. When you find reaching the high notes, and in turn the low notes, uncomfortable, you have found your "tessitura." It is your voice's comfortable range. Just for grins, try finding your own tessitura and passagio. Can you guess which voice type matches your own?

GLAUCOMA
noun
a condition of increased pressure within the eyeball, causing gradual loss of sight.

Pavarotti was, and Bocelli remains, a world-famous tenor. And what makes them so special? It is the unique combination of voice weight, tessitura, how long their voices can stay in the high notes of their range, and the way they flirt with their passagios. Pavarotti has pointed out that the tenor's performance is thrilling, even a bit dangerous. Reaching and holding the high notes creates drama and excitement.

Andrea has had an even bigger challenge in his life. Born with *glaucoma, and having suffered further injury to his eyes playing soccer at age 12, he also manages his stage appearances while being completely blind. Andrea hasn't forgotten his small-town roots in Italy. He has seen to the building of an outdoor amphitheater in Lajatico. It is called "Teatro di Silenzio," features only one concert each July for Andrea and his guest entertainers, then remains silent the rest of the year.

Teatro di Silenzio

WHAT A TRIP!

And we've just really begun to find our way through the complicated, beautiful, and amazing country of Italy. Many people return to Italy time and time again to explore what they missed along the way. There will forever be a place you have not yet seen, a fact you had not realized, a funny travel experience you will never forget. Best of all, often you meet someone new and discover you have something in common with one another.

If it weren't for this book, I would not have met YOU!

Just as insects go through "metamorphosis," shedding an outer layer or perhaps changing remarkably after a long rest inside a cozy cocoon, humans seem to go through a very similar process as they travel and consider the world they live in. Travel has the awesome ability to expand our world, change us as we grow, and help us become more mature because of what we have experienced.

Where should we go next? We'd better get buzzin'! There's so much to see, so much to do, and now I have someone to travel with me. Life is good!

For now, I think I'll take a nap. Always tired after an adventure, for sure, but it's a happy tired.

Dear Parents and Grandparents,

It is with a warm smile that I look back upon the travels we have taken with our children. Actually, even before that time.

My childhood family of seven took frequent "kitchen vacations." Imagining and discussing all took place around our kitchen table. Only two of those trips actually happened, and they remain amongst my favorite childhood memories. Truth is, it was the dreaming and planning that nurtured our wanderlust.

When I was a kid, there were no minivans, and air travel was beyond both our expectations and our budget. We just squeezed in and stored our luggage on the roof carrier or in any available nooks and crannies. I remember occasionally riding "Lincoln Log–style" with my siblings, feet, hands, arms, and legs linked together as necessary. We always broke open the cooler of snacks within an hour of our departure.

Since then . . .

My husband, Dave, has shared, even surpassed, my passion for travel. Our family moved from Wisconsin to Ohio when our youngest daughter was five. The world, at least on the east coast, had just come that much closer, within driving distance, and we tried to take full advantage. At every break from school, we packed up the car and made our way north, south, and east.

In an effort to minimize the bickering in our cramped car, I began assembling little cases of activities for each of the passenger locations in the car . . . shotgun, middle seat, and back seat of our compact station wagon. At each "pit stop," everyone would switch seats and explore a new bag of tricks.

No iPads back then!

My husband's dream was to visit his grandparents' homeland of Italy, and we planned our first European trip the year I turned 40. It was fabulous! On the long flight home, Dave planned what Italian sights he wanted to show our daughters, and we returned with them five years later. We tackled the country "kid-style," seeing 13 cities in ten days! Never enough time to linger in museums, for which they were grateful, and with only Italian programming on TV, the girls spent evenings writing in their journals and laughing together over our adventures. Priceless! Unforgettable!

Fast-forward, and three more return trips to this unique country, I still learn so much, and I still have so much more to learn. We are now the proud and doting grandparents of five, and my husband's and my passion for loving them, teaching them, and sharing in every imaginable experience remains a mission.

One obvious lesson learned is that who you are with means as much as where you go. Enter Travel Bug! If your child enjoys a plush and familiar companion, it is my hope that "T" can fill the gap and expand the value of their adventure.

For "T," I am forever grateful! My cousin, Genie Mickelson, artist, illustrator, and children's author, among other inspiring talents, created this original character. Marisa Kertscher brought him color and life. Marisa encouraged me all the way, and I am so grateful! I hope that it remains our destiny to work together again. Another huge thank you goes to my husband and our three daughters, who have encouraged me to translate my passion into this book that I have forever dreamed of writing.

Perhaps Italy is not in your sights right now, but "virtually," there are no limits on where you can go! The learning is there. The passion is there. And our children, and yours, are excited to know all about it. Even if a kitchen vacation is all you have energy for right now, DO IT!

Wishing you safe adventures and a wonderful trip!

-Katy

BIBLIOGRAPHY

Italian Language:

Italian in 10 Minutes a Day by Kristine K. Kershul
Published by Bilingual Books, Inc., 2016

Historical Perspective:

A Little History of the World by E. H. Gombrich
Published by DuMont Literatur and Kunst Verlag GmbH and Co., KG, Cologne, Germany, 1985
English translation by Caroline Mustill, 2005
Preface to the English edition by Clifford Harper, 2005

The Kingfisher Illustrated History of the World
Published by Grisewood & Dempsey Ltd., 1992
Printed in Italy
Kingfisher: Larousse Kingfisher Chambers Inc., New York, NY
First American edition, 1993

Bodies From the Ash by James M. Deem
Published by Houghton Mifflin Books for Children, an imprint of Houghton Mifflin Harcourt Publishing Co., 2005

DK Eyewitness Books: Volcano and Earthquake by Susanna Van Rose
Published by DK Penguin Random House
Most recent copyright: by Dorling Kindersley Limited in Great Britain, 2014
DK Publishing Special Markets, New York, NY

Florence, Italy: Birthplace of the Renaissance by Baby Professor
Published by Baby Professor, 2017

The Reformation: History in an Hour by Edward A. Gosselin
Published by HarperPress, 2011

Famous Men of Rome by John Haaren
First published in 1904

Insect References:

Ultimate Bug-opedia by Darlyne Murawski and Nancy Honovich
Published by National Geographic, Washington, D.C., 2013

The Illustrated world Encyclopedia of Insects by Martin Walters
Published by Lorenz Books, an imprint of Anness Publishing Ltd., London, 2014

Little Kids First Big Book of Bugs by Catherine D. Hughes
Published by National Geographic Kids, Washington, D.C., 2014

Carlo Collodi (author of *Pinocchio*):

"Carlo Collodi – The story of Pinocchio"
http://www.yourwaytoflorence.com/db/pinocchio/pinocchio.htm

Pinocchio: The Tale of a Puppet by Carlo Collodi

Sicily and its Honey:

"The taste of Sicilian honey" by Kate Ludlow, April 29, 2011
https://kateludlow.wordpress.com/2011/04/29/the-taste-of-sicilian-honey

"Sicilian Black Bee" from Slow Food Foundation for Biodiversity
https://www.fondazioneslowfood.com/en/slow-food-presidia/sicilian-black-bee/

"The Native Black Sicilian Bee Honey" by the Arte Cibo editorial board
www.artecibo.com/the-native-black-sicilian-bee-honey

"The Italian Honey Bee" by Barry Lillie, September 28, 2014
https://www.Italymagazine.com/news/Italian-honey-bee

"Carob Honey From Sicily" by Scott Pikovsky, May 6, 2014
www.greatciao.com/carobhoney/

Italian Tenors:

Andrea Bocelli:

The Music of Silence: New Edition by Andrea Bocelli
Published by Amadeus, 2011

"Andrea Bocelli," September 29, 2014, Updated: July 20, 2020
https://www.biography.com/musician/andrea-bocelli

"Andrea Bocelli"
https://www.britannica.com/biography/Andrea-Bocelli

Luciano Pavarotti:

"Luciano Pavarotti"
https://www.classicfm.com/artists/luciano-pavarotti/pictures/pavarottis-greatest-moments-gallery-highlights/

Pavarotti: My World by Luciano Pavarotti with William Wright
Published by Random House, 1996

Categories of singing voices:

"How To Determine Your Vocal Range" from Music Notes Now
https://www.musicnotes.com/now/tips/determine-vocal-range/

"Pavarotti – The Tenor Voice – If I were Only a Tenor!" Uploaded by uncjim, December 30, 2007
https://www.youtube.com/watch?v=koJMqQ5pV6E

"The 8 Singing Voice Types: Find Out Yours Here!" by Matt Ramsey, Ramsey Voice Studio, Updated September 15, 2020
https://ramseyvoice.com/voice-types/

"Tessitura"
https://www.merriam-webster.com/dictionary/tessitura

"The Dreaded Passaggio" from The Complete Singer's Resource
https://completesingers.com/technique/the-dreaded-passagio/

"Tenor"
https://www.britannica.com/art/tenor-vocal-range

Leonardo da Vinci:

"5 Revolutionary Inventions by Leonardo da Vinci" by Andrei Tapalaga, January 15, 2020
https://medium.com/history-of-yesterday/5-revolutionary-inventions-by-leonardo-da-vinci-2b555488f805

"Leonardo da Vinci: an Inventor Ahead of His Time"
https://www.da-vinci-inventions.com

Oil and Marble: A Novel of Leonardo and Michelangelo by Stephanie Storey
Published by Arcade, 2016

"Leonardi da Vinci Drawings"
https://www.leonardodavinci.net/drawings.jsp

Ferrari:

The Little Book of Ferrari by Brian Laban
Published by G2 Entertainment, 2006

Italian Inventions:

"Top Ten Italian Inventions"
http://www.italiangoodnews.com/top-ten-italian-inventions/

"Great Italian Inventions" by Francesca Bezzone, April 20, 2018, Updated: June 17, 2021
https://www.lifeinitaly.com/culture/great-italian-inventions/

Fact-checking:

"Encyclopedia Brittanica"
https://www.britannica.com/

Marble:

"Marble" from Online Etymology Dictionary
https://www.etymonline.com/word/marble

CPSIA information can be obtained
at www.ICGtesting.com
Printed in the USA
BVHW020850220921
617258BV00005B/177